This book is printed on Mohawk Superfine
Softwhite, Eggshell text
by Hall Printing Company, High Point, N.C.

The Taste of Appalachia

A Collection of Traditional Recipes
Still in Use Today

by Lyn Kellner

First Edition

Simmer Pot Press, Boone, North Carolina

THE TASTE OF APPALACHIA

A Collection of Traditional Recipes
Still in Use Today

by Lyn Kellner

Published by

Simmer Pot Press
Route 3 Box 973 A
Boone, NC 28607

Library of Congress Catalog Card No. 87–61712

ISBN 0–944010–00–8

TABLE OF CONTENTS

ACKNOWLEDGEMENTS

Many people contributed their time, talents, and efforts to the creation and production of this book.

I am deeply indebted to Rick Herrick, Ph.D., Publisher, *Quality Living;* Dee Dundon-Burke, Library Staff, Appalachian State University; Donna Houck, Ph.D., Department of English, Appalachian State University; Lillian Danner, North Carolina Agricultural Extension Service; Judy Hunt, State Representative, NC House of Representatives:

Also... Ruth Creed, Vilas, North Carolina: an extraordinary mountain cook.

And... G. W. Hayes, Jr., Dadant & Sons, Inc.

As well as special friends Grandma Ferri and Nana Jim.

Photography
by
Hank Kellner

INTRODUCTION

Generations ago, long before the Blue Ridge Parkway snaked its way through the mountains, most Appalachian settlers lived on self-contained homesteads rather than in cities or towns as we know them today. Often separated from their neighbors by miles of difficult terrain, these hardy pioneers quickly found that survival depended on their ability to make use of every available resource. What followed was a study in creative independence.

Mountain families traditionally ate what they raised on the land or gathered from the woods. As time passed, they developed a regional diet centered on available foods that were nourishing and easily prepared. Homegrown dairy products, meats, vegetables, and fruits arrived at the table in a steady stream, but overworked cooks had little time to waste turning them into fancy dishes. As a result, Appalachian homesteaders ate what is called "honest food."

Today, the hustle and bustle of modern life has invaded the mountains, and with it have come busy supermarkets and superb restaurants. Tourism has brought the outside world in, bringing with it a certain amount of prosperity to a traditionally poor area. Yet while their world spins faster than ever before, countless natives of Appalachia still cling to the simple foods that are part of their heritage.

This book contains a sampling of some of the old recipes that are still in use today. It is dedicated to the Appalachian people: to their friendly ways, smiling faces, and traditional way of life. Hopefully, it will tempt its reader to share the taste of Appalachia.

FROM THE OVEN

BUTTERMILK BISCUITS

ANGEL BISCUITS

TRADITIONAL CORNBREAD

SPOON BREAD

HUSH PUPPIES

ANNIE'S APPLE BREAD

ZUCCHINI BREAD

COUNTRY PUMPKIN BREAD

BREADS AND BISCUITS

There was a time, not so long ago, when every Appalachian cook served a hot bread three times a day. Every meal was accompanied by biscuits, corn bread, or some other steaming-hot favorite that was dipped in molasses, covered with gravy, or just buttered.

Today, mountain people still love their homemade breads even though the outside world has brought a variety of factory-baked goods to their doorstep. It's still not uncommon for a mountain woman to bake homemade biscuits for breakfast. This same woman might very well come home from work in the evening and toss a batch of cornbread into the oven while she prepares dinner.

A mountain breakfast traditionally included eggs, bacon, sausage or country ham, homefries or grits, and biscuits and gravy. If company was present, it wasn't unusual to see a platter of fried tomatoes and another of fried chicken added to this feast. Even so, if the biscuits weren't up to snuff, it was understood that the entire breakfast was a disaster.

BUTTERMILK BISCUITS

2 cups all-purpose flour
1/2 teaspoon soda
3/4 teaspoon salt
2 teaspoons baking powder
1/2 cup shortening
1–1/2 cups buttermilk

Preheat oven to 450°. Mix flour, soda, salt, and baking powder. Cut in shortening with a pastry blender. Add buttermilk and mix quickly until dough forms a ball. Turn out on a floured surface and knead a few times. Pat or roll out to a 1/2–inch thickness; then cut with a floured biscuit cutter. Bake approximately 12 minutes on an ungreased baking sheet.

Yield: approx. 15 biscuits

MILK GRAVY: Save 4 tablespoons of pan drippings (or butter) and place over low heat. Stir in 4 tablespoons flour and continue stirring until smooth and bubbly. Add 2 cups milk and stir until thickened. Salt and pepper to taste and serve piping hot.

Mountain Superstition

Wednesday is the luckiest day to be married. Saturday is the unluckiest.

In Grandma's day it was often said that a good (or bad) biscuit could make, save, or break a marriage. That'll give you a pretty good idea of how important biscuits were in the mountain scheme of things. Even today, the perfect biscuit is a source of family pride.

Angel biscuits take more time to prepare than buttermilk biscuits because they must rise before baking. Even so, they're worth the extra effort.

ANGEL BISCUITS

1 envelope dry yeast
1/4 cup warm water
5 cups self-rising flour
3 tablespoons sugar
3/4 cup shortening
2 cups buttermilk

Preheat oven to 400°. Dissolve yeast in warm water and set aside. Mix flour and sugar in mixing bowl. Cut shortening into flour mixture with a pastry blender. Add yeast and buttermilk to make a soft dough. Turn out on a floured surface and roll or pat to a 1/2–inch thickness. Cut with biscuit cutter; then place biscuits on an ungreased baking sheet. Let rise for 45 minutes; then bake for 15 minutes.

Yield: Approx. 3 dozen biscuits

Folk Remedy

To chase flies away, put a little honey into a saucer and generously sprinkle the honey with black pepper.

Corn was often called the backbone of Appalachian cooking. It was as important to the mountain diet as rice is to the Chinese. This versatile vegetable not only fed the family, but also nourished every animal in the barnyard. And when dried and ground into meal, it was used to make bread, the staff of life.

The best cornbread is made from freshly water-ground meal. Most city folks would be amazed to know how many Appalachian families still make a biweekly trip to the nearest mill.

TRADITIONAL CORNBREAD

2 cups white cornmeal
1/2 teaspoon salt
1/2 teaspoon soda
2 teaspoons baking powder
1 teaspoon sugar
1-1/4 cups buttermilk
1 egg, beaten
1/4 cup melted grease or oil

Preheat oven to 425°. Mix dry ingredients; then add buttermilk and egg. Heat grease or oil in an 8- or 9-inch skillet (until it almost smokes); then pour most of it into batter and stir. Making sure the skillet is still very hot, pour batter into it and bake for 20–25 minutes, or until nicely browned.

Yield: 6–8 servings

NOTE: Sugar has never been included in Southern cornbread except for the teaspoon or so that's used to help it brown. This is probably because this food has always been thought of as a bread, and not as a dessert.

A century ago one of the cook's biggest problems was monotony. She might have yearned to put a little variety into her family's diet, but her list of ingredients seldom, if ever, changed. She worked around this problem by baking corn pone, cracklin' bread, corn muffins, corn sticks, hoecakes, and johnny cakes. All were made from cornmeal; yet each had its own distinct taste.

Spoon bread is one of the old recipes that's still popular today. As with other traditional cornbreads, it calls for cornmeal, but its taste is quite different. It's lighter, moister, and fluffier.

SPOON BREAD

1 cup cornmeal
2–1/2 cups milk
2 tablespoons butter, melted
2 teaspoons sugar
1 teaspoon salt
2–1/2 teaspoons baking powder
3 eggs, separated

Preheat oven to 400°. Cook milk and cornmeal over medium heat, stirring constantly until thickened. Remove from heat and let cool. Add butter, sugar, salt, baking powder, and egg yolks. Beat egg whites until stiff and fold into batter. Pour into well-greased 1–1/2 quart shallow baking dish and bake for 25 minutes.

Yield: 6–8 servings

Folk Remedy

Ginseng tea made from the ginseng root will cure a colicky baby, an upset stomach, rheumatism, and even arthritis.

Many regions in the South claim to have originated the hush puppy, which is traditionally served with fish. Legend has it that a group of hunters was gathered around a campfire frying fresh-caught fish and cakes made of cornmeal. Smelling a fragrant dinner, their hounds approached the fire and bayed so loudly that the hunters tossed them bits of the cornmeal mixture saying, "Hush puppy, hush puppy."

HUSH PUPPIES

2 cups cornmeal
1/2 cup flour
2 teaspoons baking powder
1 teaspoon salt
1 cup milk
2 eggs
1/4 cup finely chopped onion

Mix cornmeal, flour, baking powder, and salt. Add milk, eggs, and onion. Stir until smooth. Drop by spoonfuls into hot fat and turn until all sides are golden brown.

Yield: about 20

Folk Remedy

Herbal teas can enhance the color of your hair: sage covers the gray in brown hair; chamomile adds golden highlights to blonde hair; henna gives a reddish glow to auburn hair.

Living in the country as they did, mountain folk knew that autumn meant apples — lots of them. And when the time came, they made great quantities of apple butter, apple cider, and applesauce.

Today you'll still find many of these foods sold at family-operated stands. And if you're lucky, you may even find apple bread made from this recipe.

ANNIE'S APPLE BREAD

1/2 cup butter or margarine
2/3 cup sugar
2 eggs, beaten
1 tablespoon lemon juice
2 cups flour
1 teaspoon baking powder
1/2 teaspoon salt
2 cups chopped apples
1 cup chopped black walnuts or pecans

Preheat oven to 350°. Cream butter, sugar, eggs, and lemon juice. Stir in flour, baking powder, and salt. Fold in apples and nuts. Bake in a greased and floured 9x5x3-inch loaf pan for 45–55 minutes.

Yield: 1 loaf

Mountain Superstition

If you find a little inchworm on your clothing, leave him be. He's just measuring you for new clothes.

15

It's interesting to note that long before the first European settlers arrived in Appalachia, American Indians were cultivating several varieties of a vegetable they called squash.

Squash, then, is about as traditional as a food can be in America. It remains popular not only as a vegetable, but also as a main ingredient in batter bread.

ZUCCHINI BREAD

3 cups flour
1 teaspoon baking powder
1 teaspoon salt
2–1/2 teaspoons cinnamon
1 cup chopped pecans
3 eggs
2 cups sugar
1 cup vegetable oil
2 teaspoons vanilla
2 cups coarsely grated raw zucchini

Preheat oven to 350°. Mix first five ingredients and set aside. In large mixing bowl, beat eggs well, then add sugar, oil, and vanilla and beat until fluffy. Stir in zucchini. Add dry ingredients and stir just until moistened. Place batter in two well-greased 9x5–inch loaf pans and bake for one hour.

Yield: 2 loaves

Mountain Superstition

The number of fogs in August determines the number of snowfalls during the following winter.

16

In the old days the pumpkin was cultivated as food for stock, as a vegetable, and as the chief ingredient in pumpkin pie. Needless to say, this large member of the squash family never went to waste.

Today most city people associate pumpkin with Thanksgiving Day, but mountain people enjoy its unique taste year round. It's delicious not only in pies, but also in cakes and breads.

COUNTRY PUMPKIN BREAD

3/4 cup shortening
2–1/2 cups sugar
4 eggs, beaten
2 cups cooked pumpkin
2/3 cup water
3–1/2 cups all-purpose flour
1/2 teaspoon baking powder
2 teaspoons soda
1 teaspoon salt
1 teaspoon cinnamon
1 teaspoon allspice
1 cup black walnuts
2/3 cup raisins

Preheat oven to 350°. Cream shortening, sugar, and eggs. Stir in pumpkin and water. Mix together flour, baking powder, soda, salt, and spices. Stir dry ingredients into wet ingredients. Fold in nuts and raisins. Spoon batter into two greased and floured 9x5-inch loaf pans and bake for one hour, or until bread tests done with a toothpick.

Yield: 2 loaves

Folk Remedy

Honey applied to bee stings will stop the pain.

APPALACHIAN MAIN MEALS

COUNTRY HAM AND RED-EYE GRAVY

HAM AND RICE SKILLET DINNER

ROAST PORK WITH SAUERKRAUT

APPALACHIAN MEAT LOAF

SOUTHERN FRIED CHICKEN

EASY CHICKEN POT PIE

SUMMER VEGETABLE DINNER

OLD TIMEY POTATO SOUP

WHAT'S FOR DINNER?

Back in Grandma's day when the family gathered for a main meal, chances were the meat on the table would be either chicken or pork. These meats were served most often because they were readily available. Chickens thrived in the barnyard, and an annual hog slaughtering kept the smokehouse filled with preserved bacon, salt pork, and ham.

In the summer when fresh produce was plentiful, dinner might be a combination of a half dozen vegetables cooked in various ways. Homegrown beans, potatoes, and a colorful assortment of vegetables that were picked and eaten the same day were marvelous sources of protein, carbohydrates, and vitamins.

Beef was the least favored meat, and for good reason. Because there was no refrigeration in the old days, freshly slaughtered beef had to be eaten fresh or preserved in canning jars. That seems like a lot of trouble for what must have been a tasteless source of protein.

Country ham has been the pride of Appalachia for generations. Carefully cured over hickory fires, this ham was seasoned in a smokehouse for at least a year until it was covered with a white-speckled mold. Only then was it considered ready for the table.

To bring out the unique flavor of country ham, always slice it thin. Then, if you want to prepare a true mountain meal, fry it, cover it with red-eye gravy, and serve it with homemade hot buttered biscuits and a jar of sourwood honey.

COUNTRY HAM AND RED-EYE GRAVY

Slice ham about 1/4 inch thick. Heat a cast iron skillet, add about a tablespoon of grease, and fry ham on both sides only long enough to brown it. Remove ham to a warm platter. Now add about 1/2 cup of water to pan drippings and stir until the gravy sizzles. Pour over ham and serve.

NOTE: Some people add a couple of teaspoons of strong coffee to the gravy to give it color. Other people will tell you it's a sacrilege to do so. It all depends on whom you ask.

Historical Note

While folk hero Daniel Boone was out hunting one evening, he saw a pair of eyes shining in the darkness. His quarry ran from him, and he chased it. But what he thought was a deer turned out to be a young woman named Rebecca Bryan. Soon afterward, Rebecca became Daniel's wife.

A hundred years ago most mountain women didn't have the luxury of tending just the house and the garden. Instead, they often spent their days working beside their husbands in the fields. At the end of the day, these tired women still had to prepare nourishing meals. Using three of their favorite ingredients, ham, rice, and cheddar cheese, they could put dinner on the table in a matter of minutes.

HAM AND RICE SKILLET DINNER

2 cups cooked rice
1 cup diced smoked shoulder ham
1 small onion, diced
Salt, pepper, and generous sprinkling of paprika
1 to 1-1/4 cups shredded cheddar cheese

Fry onion in a few teaspoons of oil. Add spices, ham, and stir in rice. Stir in cheese and cover until cheese melts. Serve with cornbread and a nice green vegetable.

Yield: 2 servings

Interesting Phenomenon

Foxfire is an interesting mountain phenomenon. Because it glows in the dark with a cool, blue luminous light, it was once believed to be a fairy light, something truly magic. But now scientists tell us that foxfire is a light given off by fungi that grow in damp, rotting places like tree stumps and stream banks.

There was a time when a freshly-slaughtered pig meant that a juicy loin of pork would soon appear on the Sunday dinner table. This roast would probably be served with a bowl of crisp sauerkraut, mounds of mashed potatoes, plenty of greens, and steaming hot biscuits.

As time passes, more and more families are buying pork from well-stocked supermarket display cases. Folks readily admit, though, that the taste isn't what it used to be.

ROAST PORK WITH SAUERKRAUT

1 4–6 pound pork loin roast
1 tablespoon garlic powder
1 tablespoon paprika
2 teaspoons salt
1 teaspoon pepper
1 tablespoon vinegar
2–1/2 pounds canned sauerkraut

Day before: Mix a paste of garlic powder, paprika, salt, pepper, and vinegar. Rub all of paste over the roast. Cover and store in refrigerator until an hour before cooking.

Preheat oven to 325°. Place roast on a rack in shallow roasting pan. Add 1–1/2 cups water to the pan. Cook uncovered for 35–40 minutes per pound, or until meat thermometer registers 170°. Baste and turn roast several times while cooking. Keep it moist.

One-half hour before roast is done, remove from oven and pour off fat, leaving all brown drippings in pan. Put roast back in pan, add 1/2 cup of water, and lay sauerkraut in around the roast. Turn sauerkraut once or twice during next 1/2 hour so it will absorb flavor from drippings.

Yield: 8–10 servings

Beef wasn't popular in the mountains until after the Second World War when America went through a tremendous growth spurt and supermarkets came to Appalachia. Even though meat loaf began to make frequent appearances by that time, it was still flavored with the traditional taste of pork sausage. To those who have never tried it, this combination of meats will come as a nice change.

APPALACHIAN MEAT LOAF

1-1/2 pounds ground chuck
1 pound ground pork breakfast sausage
1-1/2 cups cooked rice
1 teaspoon salt
1/2 teaspoon pepper

Preheat oven to 350°. Mix ingredients together and lightly press into a 9x5-inch loaf pan. The top of the loaf should be flat to make an even surface for the sauce topping.

SWEET AND SOUR TOPPING

1/2 cup ketchup
1/4 cup brown sugar
1-1/2 teaspoons dry mustard

Mix together and pour over the top of the meat loaf. Bake 1 hour, 15 minutes.

Yield: 6 servings

Mountain Superstition

If your man is thinking of leaving you for another woman, wedge a lock of his hair in the door jamb, and his wanderings will cease.

Unexpected company was never much of a problem for mountain women who kept chickens in the barnyard. All they had to do was hurry outside and catch a couple of fat birds for dinner.

It's said that Southern fried chicken is one of the world's best-kept secrets. Not so! Using the right bird and the right technique, it's easy to fry chicken that's crisp and golden on the outside and tender on the inside.

SOUTHERN FRIED CHICKEN

9–10 pieces of fresh chicken (never frozen)
2 cups buttermilk (to tenderize and flavor)
Lard or oil (soybean, peanut, or corn)
1 tablespoon bacon grease (optional)
1–1/2 cups flour
2 teaspoons salt
1 teaspoon pepper

Wash chicken in cold water, dry with paper towels, place in a large bowl, and add buttermilk. Turn all pieces to coat with buttermilk and place in refrigerator for one hour.

Chicken is crispiest when fried in 2 inches of oil. Heat oil to between 350° and 360°. This is the right temperature to brown the outside while sealing moisture inside. Bacon grease can be added at this time to add flavor.

Remove chicken from buttermilk and dredge in the mixture of flour, salt, and pepper. Place in hot oil. Cover to seal in moisture. Chicken should be turned just once while cooking. Turn with tongs, not with a fork. Fry 10 minutes on the first side and 15 minutes on the second side. Drain on paper towels and serve piping hot.

Yield: 4–5 servings

In Appalachian households, chicken pot pie has always been an excellent remedy for leftover chicken. With the addition of gravy, peas, and topping, yesterday's chicken could easily form the basis for today's main meal. Served with a salad and fruit, the leftover bird made for a quick and tasty dinner.

EASY CHICKEN POT PIE

Filling:
- 4 tablespoons butter
- 4 tablespoons flour
- 2 cups chicken broth (fresh or canned)
- 2 cups chicken, cooked and diced
- 2 cups green peas
- Salt and pepper to taste

Topping:
- 1/2 cup butter, melted
- 1 cup self-rising flour
- 1 cup milk

FILLING: Preheat oven to 425°. Melt butter in a 2-quart saucepan. Do not burn. Add flour and stir until smooth and bubbly. Stirring constantly, slowly add chicken broth and cook over medium heat until sauce thickens. Add chicken and peas. Pour into a 1-1/2 quart shallow baking dish.

TOPPING: Place flour in a small bowl. Add melted butter and milk. Stir and spread over chicken mixture. Bake for 25–30 minutes, or until topping browns and filling is hot.

Yield: 4–6 servings

Folk Remedy

Take nine gulps of water to cure the hiccups; then walk backwards nine steps.

26

Even though mountain people have always loved chicken and pork, there must have been times in the past when the daily appearance of these two meats became monotonous. When that happened, it was time for a colorful vegetable dinner. In the late summer, when fresh vegetables could be picked and eaten in the same day, they provided a feast for the eye as well as for the palate.

SUMMER VEGETABLE DINNER

2 large tomatoes, diced
1 green pepper, diced
1 cup onions, sliced
2 cups yellow summer squash, sliced
1 cup Monterey Jack cheese, grated
Salt, pepper, and crushed dill weed to taste

Place vegetables in a steamer basket into large saucepan. Add about 1 inch of water to saucepan and bring to a boil. Cover and simmer until vegetables are almost tender (approx. 10 minutes). Place cooked vegetables in a large bowl, season to taste, and sprinkle grated cheese on top. Serve with mounds of mashed potatoes or pinto beans, fresh corn on the cob, and a couple of zippy relishes.

Yield: 4 servings

Folk Remedy

Use a sliver of wood from a lightning-struck tree to cure a toothache.

Times could be hard in the old days, but if a cow was in the barnyard and potatoes and onions were stored in the root cellar, then a hearty soup supper was always possible. Served with cornbread and a dish of home-canned fruit, this supper has long been a winter favorite in the mountains.

OLD TIMEY POTATO SOUP

1 medium onion, minced
1/4 cup butter
4 cups diced raw potatoes
2 cups water
1 teaspoon salt
4 cups milk
Few dashes celery seed
Salt and pepper to taste
4 slices bacon, cooked and
**   crumbled (optional)**

Sauté onion in butter until translucent. Add potatoes, water, and salt, and cook until tender. Add milk and season to taste. Simmer a few minutes before serving.

Yield: 6–8 servings

Folk Remedy

To prevent poison ivy, eat a little of the root of the plant, and you'll be immune all summer.

VEGETABLES AND SIDE DISHES

GRANDMA'S SWEET POTATOES

MIXED SOUTHERN GREENS

CORN PUDDING

FRIED OKRA

GREEN TOMATO DUO

GLAZED CARROTS

CREED FREEZER SLAW

FRIED APPLES

EVER BEEN IN A ROOT CELLAR?

A root cellar is a room in which food is stored. It can be either a space under a building or an area dug into the side of a hill. For centuries root cellars have been perfect places to store food because they're cold and dark; yet they never freeze. Most city dwellers would be amazed to know that a surprisingly large number of root cellars are still in use in Appalachia today.

When you open the door to a root cellar dug into the side of a hill, sunlight rushes past you, travels across an earthen floor, and zeroes in on hundreds of twinkling glass jars. It's a kaleidoscope of taste and color. Beans, peas, peaches, pears, corn, tomatoes, pickled beets, relishes, cherries and berries, and even homemade sauerkraut sit on wooden shelves in long, neat rows. On the floor are wooden bins filled with potatoes and onions, and in the corner a burlap bag overflows with the bulbous roots of last year's dahlia plants, stored where frost cannot reach them.

Come spring, the flowers will be replanted along with another vegetable garden, and the cycle will begin again. In the mountains tradition has a way of renewing itself.

In the mountains there were always as many sweet potato recipes as there were cooks. Sweet potatoes were one vegetable that could be boiled, baked, whipped, or souffléed and always come out a winner.

The following recipe will produce sweet potatoes that are delicious on the day they're cooked ...and even better when reheated the next day.

GRANDMA'S SWEET POTATOES

2–3 pounds sweet potatoes, fresh cooked
or canned
6 tablespoons butter, melted
1/2 cup brown sugar
1/3 cup honey or pancake syrup
1 teaspoon cinnamon
1 teaspoon vanilla

Preheat oven to 350°. If using canned potatoes, drain well. Slice potatoes 1 inch thick and lay in the bottom of a 9x13-inch baking pan. Mix rest of ingredients and pour over potatoes. Bake for 30 minutes, turning once or twice. If a thicker syrup is desired, bake longer.

Yield: 6–8 servings

Mountain Superstition

A singing cricket on the hearth will bring you good luck. But if you kill the cricket, the good luck will go elsewhere.

Years ago the word *greens* never meant one specific kind of green. It could have meant turnip greens, kale, chard, spinach, poke sallet, collards, mustard, or even dandelion greens. And this is still true today.

Each of these greens has its own flavor, but all are prepared with pork neck bones, ham hocks, salt pork, or bacon. The meats are used only to flavor the greens.

MIXED SOUTHERN GREENS

**5 pounds of a mixture of mustard and
    turnip greens
2 pounds ham hocks
2 quarts water
1 teaspoon crushed red pepper
Salt and pepper to taste
Vinegar**

In a large pot cover the ham hocks with 2 quarts water. Boil for 1 hour. In the meantime remove stems and wash greens several times in cold water until you're sure all sand is removed. Add greens to the pot, along with peppers and salt. If turnips are attached to the greens, peel, dice and throw them in too. Boil for 30 minutes, or until greens are tender. Serve with vinegar on the side.

Yield: 10 servings

NOTE: An added feature of the recipe is "pot likker," the liquid that remains in the pot after the greens are removed. Far too nutritious to throw away, it's placed on the table in separate bowls. Now, for the sake of tradition, serve hot, buttered cornbread to dunk in the pot likker. That's Applachian!

"Heap high the farmer's wintry hoard!/Heap high the golden corn!/No richer gift has autumn poured/From out her lavish horn!" So wrote the poet Whittier in *The Corn Song.* Although it would be nice to think that Whittier was inspired by corn pudding, most likely he wasn't. But who can say for sure? Maybe he was.

CORN PUDDING

2 tablespoons butter, melted
3 eggs, beaten
2 tablespoons onion, minced
2 tablespoons sugar
1 teaspoon salt
1 16–ounce can cream style corn
1–1/3 cups half-and-half
> **or**
2 small cans evaporated milk

Preheat oven to 350°. Mix all ingredients, adding corn and cream last. Turn into a buttered 2–quart casserole. Bake casserole in a pan of water about 1 inch deep for 1 hour.

Yield: 6 servings

NOTE: Corn pudding can also be made with 2 cups of fresh or frozen corn, but 2 tablespoons of flour must be added to thicken it.

Mountain Superstition

If you put your clothing on inside out by mistake, you'll have a lucky day.

Long ago, mountain cooks discovered that some vegetables, like green tomatoes, squash, and okra, could be coated and fried. The crunchy taste of the fried side dish added a little something extra to what might have been a nothing-special meal.

Today okra is so popular in the mountains that regional restaurants wouldn't dream of leaving it off their menus. Even fast-food restaurants include bowls of okra at their vegetable and salad bars.

FRIED OKRA

**1 pound okra, fresh or frozen,
cut into 1/2-inch slices
2 eggs
1/3 cup milk
1-1/2 cups yellow cornmeal
Salt and pepper to taste**

Heat 1 inch of vegetable oil in a skillet. Beat eggs and milk together in one bowl, and stir cornmeal, salt, and pepper together in another. Dip okra first in egg mixture; then coat with cornmeal. Drop into hot oil and fry until golden (okra will float to the surface). Drain on paper towels and place in a warm oven until ready to serve.

Yield: 4 servings

Interesting Phenomenon

The tiny brilliant lights that appear on Brown Mountain in North Carolina have never been scientifically explained. First seen during the 18th Century, the lights appear just after dark, bob from place to place, and then disappear.

Oldtimers who planted vegetable gardens knew there were two times when green tomatoes were picked: at the beginning of the season when folks just couldn't wait any longer for the tomatoes to ripen; and at the end of the season when frost threatened to wither what was left on the vine. But when they prepared fried tomatoes sprinkled with plenty of pepper, they probably found themselves picking green tomatoes during mid season as well.

GREEN TOMATO DUO

3–4 medium-sized green tomatoes
3/4 cup yellow cornmeal
1 teaspoon salt
1/2 teaspoon black pepper
1 egg, beaten

FRY THEM: Slice tomatoes 1/2 inch thick. Dip first in beaten egg; then in cornmeal, salt, and pepper mixture. Fry in hot oil until nicely browned on both sides.

or

BAKE THEM: Instead of frying, place a single layer of meal-coated tomatoes on a buttered baking tin. Bake at 425° for 30–35 minutes, turning once. Delicious with grated cheddar or parmesan cheese sprinkled on top.

Yield: 6 servings

NOTE: In the mountains green tomatoes are popular not only as a dinner vegetable, but also as a breakfast side dish.

Mountain Superstition

Never keep peacock feathers in the house: they bring disastrous bad luck.

In earlier years carrots were grown for animal fodder. Now, of course, they're a popular "people" food that can be prepared in dozens of ways to enhance their flavor. Nutmeg, ginger, or thyme will complement the colorful carrot, as will mint or white sauce or a dash of horseradish. In the mountains glazed carrots have long been a favorite.

GLAZED CARROTS

1 pound carrots
2 tablespoons butter
2/3 cup chicken broth or water
Salt and pepper
1-1/2 teaspoons sugar

Peel carrots and slice into 1-inch pieces. Melt butter in a skillet, add carrots, and move them around a bit to coat them. Add broth, salt, and pepper. Cover and cook for 20 minutes or until there is very little liquid left in pan. Add sugar and move the carrots around in the pan until they glaze.

Yield: 4 servings

NOTE: If your prefer to glaze carrots with honey, try a honey butter sauce. Beat 1/2 cup butter and 1/2 cup honey until fluffy and add a teaspoon of orange or lemon rind. Pour over cooked carrots and serve immediately.

Mountain Superstition

If you make a wish as soon as you walk through the door of a new home, your wish will come true.

Some people wonder why so many Appalachian cooks still take the time to preserve their own jams, jellies, pickles, and relishes. Well, if the ingredients are accessible and the heart and mind are willing, why not? But the real reason, of course, is that home canning is another one of those traditions that adds to the quality of life.

CREED FREEZER SLAW

1 medium cabbage, shredded
1 teaspoon salt
1 carrot, grated
1 green pepper, chopped fine
1 cup vinegar
1/4 cup water
1 teaspoon mustard seed
1-1/2 cups sugar
1 teaspoon celery seed

Add salt to shredded cabbage, set aside for one hour, then drain. Stir carrot and green pepper into cabbage. In a large saucepan make a syrup of vinegar, water, mustard seed, sugar, and celery seed. Boil for one minute and remove from heat. When the syrup has cooled to lukewarm, pour it over the cabbage mixture and stir well. Spoon slaw into one-pint plastic containers. Refrigerate until cold; then transfer to freezer.

Yield: 4–5 pints

Folk Remedy

Soot gathered from a fireplace will help a wound stop bleeding.

Fried apples weren't actually fried: they were steamed in a covered skillet. A wide skillet surface allowed the mountain cook to handle the apples without turning them into applesauce.

Dozens of apple dishes, including apple fritters, applesauce, and fried apples have always been popular in the mountains, probably because they're so good with ham and pork. Even today, these side dishes often appear on the table at area restaurants, whether they're requested or not.

FRIED APPLES

**4–5 firm apples, cored and quartered
(leave skins on)
1 cup water
1/3 cup sugar
1/2 cup orange juice
1 teaspoon cinnamon**

Put water, sugar, orange juice, and cinnamon in a wide skillet and bring to a boil. Simmer for 5 minutes; then add apples and cover. Turning the apples once or twice, cook them until they are tender, about 20 minutes.

NOTE: The combination of citrus, apple, and cinnamon will make your kitchen a fragrant place in which to work.

Historical Note

The original inhabitants of Appalachia were the Apalachee Indians. When Hernando DeSoto explored the area during the 16th Century, his men named the mountains after them.

EGGS AND CHEESE

FARMHOUSE OMELET

DEVILED EGGS

CHEESE GRITS SOUFFLÉ

JESSIE'S MACARONI AND CHEESE

AU GRATIN POTATOES

THINGS WERE DIFFERENT IN THE OLD DAYS

Believe it or not, there was a time when people ate eggs and cheese with a clear conscience. Country families sat down to huge omelet breakfasts with grits and biscuits swimming in butter. Then they left the table and went off to the fields for long hours of hard physical labor.

Because they had never heard of it, these people didn't worry about cholesterol. Moreover, they never knew that physical activity burned off their fatty foods as fast as they consumed them. So in blissful ignorance — and barring accidental death — many of them lived for a hundred years.

Today we function in a sedentary society that's prone to clogged arteries. We consciously keep track of how many eggs we eat each week, and we visit health spas and gyms instead of working our calories off naturally, as country families did years ago.

Things sure were different in the old days!

An omelet could take care of most of the ingredients in a mountain family's breakfast, but grits, gravy, homemade biscuits, and honey would also appear on the traditional breakfast table.

Later, after a hearty breakfast, the family would leave the house to work for a few hours before returning for a midday main meal.

FARMHOUSE OMELET

6–8 eggs, well beaten
6 strips bacon
1 small onion
4 cooked potatoes, cubed

Fry bacon until crisp. Set aside. Leave enough bacon grease in skillet to fry onion and potatoes until tender. Add eggs and crumbled bacon. Stir and cover. Cook only until set. Salt and pepper to taste and serve piping hot.

Yield: 4 servings

Mountain Superstition

If you leave your house to journey somewhere and find that you've forgotten something, never reenter the house unless you walk through the door backwards. If you walk forward, you'll have bad luck.

Because chickens were in every barnyard and eggs were plentiful, there were few old-time mountain gatherings that lacked a platter of deviled eggs. Even today, every church supper or family gathering always includes a few versions of this old favorite.

DEVILED EGGS

8 hardboiled eggs
1 teaspoon dry mustard
1/4 cup mayonnaise
Salt and pepper
3 tablespoons finely minced celery
3 tablespoons finely minced ham or
cooked bacon

Cut hardboiled eggs in half, slip out yolks and mash with a fork. Mix in the rest of the ingredients and fill egg whites with the yolk mixture. Sprinkle with paprika and arrange on a bed of greens.

NOTE: As a substitute for the ham or bacon, you might want to try shrimp, lobster, or crabmeat as fillers.

Mountain Superstition

When you have guests you want to be rid of, stand a broom behind the door or sprinkle salt behind their chairs. If you don't want them ever to return, throw salt after them when they leave.

Other parts of America might have adopted many different kinds of cheeses, but in the mountains the words *cheese* and *cheddar* have always been synonymous.

Even today, if you wander through one of our grocery stores, stop for a moment and check the contents of the dairy case. You'll notice that about two-thirds of the cheese you'll see is some form of cheddar.

CHEESE GRITS SOUFFLÉ

1 cup uncooked grits
8 ounces cheddar cheese, grated
1/2 cup butter or margarine, melted
2 eggs, well beaten
1/4 cup milk
Salt and pepper to taste

Preheat oven to 350°. Cook grits according to package instructions. While grits are still hot, add the rest of the ingredients and stir until the cheese melts. Spoon into a lightly greased 1–1/2 quart casserole and bake for 1 hour.

Yield: 6 servings

NOTE: For a fluffier soufflé, add only yolks to the hot mixture. Beat egg whites until stiff and fold them in last.

Folk Remedy

Make a weak brew of catnip tea to ease a baby that has colic. A stronger brew will ease chest congestion in adults.

45

Macaroni and cheese has long been a favorite dish in all Southern states, not just in the mountains. Although it is the perfect complement to all kinds of meat, it can also stand alone as a main dish with a vegetable or salad dinner. This recipe goes back to a time when the family cow provided the milk that was made into cottage cheese.

JESSIE'S MACARONI AND CHEESE

1 half-pound package elbow macaroni
1 cup sour cream
2 cups cottage cheese
1/2 cup milk
1 egg, beaten
1/2 pound processed cheese food
        or
        cheddar cheese, grated
1/2 teaspoon salt
1/4 teaspoon pepper

Preheat oven to 350°. Cook macaroni according to package directions. While macaroni cooks, combine the rest of the ingredients in a large bowl. Drain macaroni and add to cheese mixture. Stir until well mixed; then pour into a greased 2–quart casserole. Bake about 40 minutes, or until bubbly and slightly browned.

Yield: 6–8 servings

Folk Remedy

To relieve a sprained ankle, wrap it in brown paper soaked with vinegar.

When the family root cellar was bulging with a new crop of potatoes, it was up to the farm wife to find a few new ways to glorify the humble spud. She would have added cheddar cheese, of course, but today the use of muenster or processed cheese food will yield a creamier texture and taste.

One of the nicest things about au gratin potatoes is that with the addition of a layer of leftover meat or vegetables, it can become a one-dish meal.

AU GRATIN POTATOES

4 cups very thinly sliced raw potatoes
1 thinly sliced onion
1/2 pound diced cheese of your choice
Milk
Salt and pepper to taste

Preheat oven to 350°. Grease a shallow 1-1/2 quart casserole. Place a thin layer of potatoes in the bottom of the casserole, then a layer of onions, then cheese. Continue to layer until all ingredients are used. Pour milk over layers until the casserole is about 2/3 full. Add salt and pepper. Bake for 50 minutes, or until potatoes are easily pierced with a fork.

Yield: 4–6 servings

Folk Remedy

In the old days, a snake bite might have been treated with one or more of the following: salt, gunpowder, ammonia, turpentine, sugar, kerosene, vinegar, and possibly even an onion.

HOMECOMING DESSERTS

CAROLINA GINGERBREAD

HONEY APPLE PIE

NO-MIX BLACKBERRY COBBLER

NANA JIM'S RICE PUDDING

COLD OVEN POUND CAKE

HOMEMADE BANANA PUDDING

PECAN PIE

CHOCOLATE PECAN PIE

HONEY, MOLASSES, AND SUGAR

Years ago when white sugar was either unavailable or very expensive, mountain cooks were forced to adopt other sweeteners. They started bee hives for honey, and they planted sugar cane patches on every homestead. When the cane was ready to be harvested, it was usually a time for celebration. Neighbors gathered at a community press where they first squeezed the juice from the cane before boiling it for hours until it became a dark, thick molasses. It took approximately ten gallons of cane juice to make one gallon of molasses.

As time passed, white sugar became plentiful, and most of the old recipes, including the ones in this book, were updated to make use of it. The benefit of sugar was that it was sweet, yet virtually flavorless, while the unique taste of honey or molasses lent too strong a flavor to many dishes.

Interestingly, the pendulum seems to be in motion again. Nutritionists tell us, for example, that we eat too many over-processed foods like sugar. They tell us, also, to return to purer foods like honey and molasses. The irony here is that prices have done a flip-flop: honey and molasses are now more expensive than sugar.

Back when molasses was plentiful and sugar wasn't, early settlers realized that if they couldn't subdue the strong taste of molasses, then the next best solution would be to complement it. Because ginger is the perfect complement to molasses, gingerbread made frequent appearances on the mountain table.

CAROLINA GINGERBREAD

1/2 cup sugar
1/2 cup butter
2 eggs
1 cup molasses
2-3/4 cups flour
1/2 teaspoon salt
2 teaspoons soda
1 teaspoon ginger
1 teaspoon cinnamon
1 cup buttermilk

Preheat oven to 350°. Cream sugar, butter, and eggs. Add molasses. Sift together flour, salt, soda, and spices. Stir dry ingredients into moist ingredients, alternating with buttermilk. Bake in a greased 9-inch square pan for 30-40 minutes.

Yield: 9 servings

Mountain Superstition

A rainbow in the morning means that bad weather is coming, but a rainbow in the evening means that clear weather is ahead.

If sugar wasn't available and molasses was too strong, that left the mountain cook with only one way to sweeten an apple pie — honey. It was soon discovered that honey complements the taste of apples the same way molasses complements gingerbread.

HONEY APPLE PIE

Pastry for an 8-inch double crust pie
6 cups sliced tart apples
1-1/2 cups honey
1-1/2 tablespoons lemon juice
1/4 cup flour
1 teaspoon cinnamon
1-1/2 tablespoons butter or margarine
1/2 cup chopped black walnuts (optional)

Roll out bottom crust and place in an 8-inch pie pan. Arrange apple slices over pastry. Mix honey, lemon juice, and flour, and pour over apples. Sprinkle with cinnamon and dot with butter. Cover with top crust and seal edges. Cut steam vents in top crust and bake at 425° for 40 minutes, or until apples are tender.

Yield: 6-8 servings

Mountain Superstition

It's bad luck if a black cat crosses your path, but good luck if a squirrel does.

When summer rolled around, it was time for the mountain family to head for the nearest blackberry thicket. Soon enough, there would be jams and jellies, juicy pies, and canning jars filled with dark, glistening berries. But first there would be blackberry cobbler, a dish as synonymous with summertime as kids in a swimming hole and flowers in a garden.

NO-MIX BLACKBERRY COBBLER

> 2 cups fresh blackberries
> 1/2 cup sugar
> 6 teaspoons butter
> 3/4 cup flour
> 1 cup sugar
> 2 teaspoons baking powder
> 1/2 teaspoon salt
> 3/4 cup milk

Preheat oven to 350°. Stir 1/2 cup sugar into fruit and set aside. Melt butter in baking pan. Sift next four ingredients together, then add milk. Pour batter into pan of melted butter, but *do not mix!* Pour fruit over batter, but *do not mix!* Bake for 50 minutes.

Yield: 6 servings

Mountain Superstition

Soap should be made only at the time of a full moon. If it's made at any other time, it won't harden.

53

Many of the mountain country's earliest settlers came from the British Isles; therefore, it's not surprising that rice pudding came with them. It seems that this simple, nourishing, and flavorful dessert has never lost its appeal to mountain palates. In fact, this pudding is still served quite frequently in area restaurants.

NANA JIM'S RICE PUDDING

1/4 cup uncooked rice
1/2 cup salted water
3 eggs, beaten
3-1/2 cups milk
1/4 cup sugar
1 teaspoon vanilla
1/4 teaspoon nutmeg
1/2 cup raisins (optional)

Preheat oven to 350°. Cook rice in salted water until moisture is absorbed. Mix eggs, milk, sugar, and vanilla. Add cooked rice to milk mixture and pour into 1-1/2 quart casserole. Sprinkle nutmeg on top. Place casserole in a pan of water and bake for 45 minutes.

Yield: 6 servings

Mountain Superstition

If two people share a towel to dry their hands, they'll be friends forever.

Hundreds of years ago, this recipe called for one pound each of butter, flour, eggs, and sugar — hence, the name pound cake. Today, pound cake is an established tradition, not only in the mountains, but all over the South.

There's a reason for starting a pound cake in a cold oven: the entire cake rises evenly, and the result is a level top. But if you prefer a cake with a high center and lower sides, bake it in a preheated oven for approximately the same length of time.

COLD OVEN POUND CAKE

1–1/2 cups butter at room temperature
3 cups sugar
5 eggs
3 cups sifted all-purpose flour
1–1/4 cups milk
1–1/2 teaspoons vanilla
1 teaspoon lemon flavoring

Cream butter and sugar until light and fluffy. Add eggs one at a time, beating well after each addition. Add flour alternately with milk. Add flavorings and beat at medium speed for 4–5 minutes. Pour batter into a greased and floured 10–inch tube pan and place in a cold oven. Set temperature for 325° and bake for 1 hour 20 minutes, or until cake tests done.

Yield: 16 servings

NOTE: It's important to beat pound cake batter very well because other than air, there are no ingredients to help it rise.

It was indeed a rare occasion when an old–time family celebration, church supper, or community gathering didn't include banana pudding, the all-around best-loved dessert in the mountains.

Even today the homemade variety still enjoys great popularity. Try this recipe and you'll lose your taste for instant pudding.

HOMEMADE BANANA PUDDING

2 eggs, plus two egg yolks
2/3 cup sugar
3 tablespoons flour
2 cups milk
1 tablespoon butter
1 teaspoon vanilla
Vanilla wafers
4–5 bananas, sliced
2 egg whites
1/4 teaspoon cream of tartar
2 tablespoons sugar

Preheat oven to 375°. Beat eggs and yolks well; then add sugar and flour. Place milk in the top of a double boiler. Add egg mixture to milk and simmer for approximately 15 minutes, stirring constantly. When mixture thickens, remove from heat and stir in butter and vanilla.

Place a layer of vanilla wafers in the bottom of a deep 2–quart baking dish. Cover wafers with a layer of sliced bananas, then a layer of custard. Continue layering, ending with custard. Beat egg whites until peaks form. Add sugar and cream of tartar and continue beating. Meringue should hold a peak but not be dry. Spread meringue over the top of the pudding to seal the edges. Bake 10 minutes, or until the topping is golden brown.

Yield: 6 servings

No one has ever claimed that the pecan pie originated in the mountains; nevertheless, it has always enjoyed much popularity.

The following recipes are but two of hundreds of possibilities. Both are easy to prepare, very rich, and very good.

PECAN PIE

1 unbaked 9-inch pie shell
1/3 cup butter, melted
1 cup brown sugar, firmly packed
3 eggs
1 cup light corn syrup
1 teaspoon vanilla
A pinch of salt
1-1/2 cups broken pecans

Preheat oven to 350°. Cream butter and sugar, then add eggs. Stir in corn syrup, vanilla, salt, and pecans. Pour into a 9-inch unbaked shell and bake for 40–50 minutes, or until firm. Serve with whipped cream.

Yield: 8–10 servings

Mountain Superstition

Hold a mirror over a spring on the first day of May, and you'll see the face of your future sweetheart.

CHOCOLATE PECAN PIE

1 large or 2 small unbaked pie shells
2 squares unsweetened baking chocolate
1/4 cup butter
1 cup light corn syrup
3/4 cup sugar
3 eggs
1 teaspoon vanilla
1–1/2 cups broken pecans

Preheat oven to 375°. Melt chocolate and butter in double boiler. Set aside. Boil syrup and sugar for about 2 minutes. Add chocolate mixture to syrup mixture. Beat eggs well; then slowly add hot mixture to eggs, beating constantly. Add vanilla and nuts. Pour into unbaked pie shell. Bake 45–50 minutes.

Yield: 1 large or two small pies

Mountain Superstition

Those who sing before breakfast will cry before supper.

Folk Remedy

To stop bleeding and to help a cut heal, gather cobwebs and apply them to the wound.

INDEX

For information about beautiful, high-quality reproductions of the photographs in this book, write the publisher.

My Favorite Recipes

My Favorite Recipes